# Cycling: HIIT Bike Training

## A Simple Proven Guide to Getting Faster & Stronger Using High Intensity Interval Bike Workouts Today

# Table of Contents

# Introduction: It's Time to HIIT the Road

I want to thank you and congratulate you for downloading the book Cycling: HIIT Bike Training.

This book contains proven steps and strategies on how to truly integrate High Intensity Interval Training into your bicycle workout routine. It doesn't matter if you are a beginner or a seasoned health buff. As long as you have the right equipment and the determination, you will be able to reach your workout goals using the HIIT regimen.

Here's an inescapable fact: you will need to get in shape to have a happy life. Having all the money and time in the world will not be enjoyable if you are not healthy. It's time to let go of your excuses and start taking control of your fitness and your happiness. This book will teach you how to lose weight and gain muscles using the HIIT system. This system is designed for people who hate the monotony of regular workout routines. It can also be adjusted to fit your health conditions and your fitness level. This book particularly advocates using the HIIT system with cycling to gain the maximum effects of the system. Compared to running, cycling creates significantly less amount of stress to your knees. It also allows you to see more places.

If you do not develop your workout routine using the HIIT system, the monotony of steady-state endurance workouts will bore you into submission. Many athletes get tired of this monotony and some even abandon their workout habit altogether. HIIT is not the type of workout where you need to grind it out for hour just to lose the weight you gained in last night's meal. In the HIIT system, you will use different levels of workout intensity in your cycling sessions. The high intensity effort will help you burn more calories in a shorter period of time. This is the reason why the HIIT system has shorter workout sessions compared to other endurance routines.

Combining the principles of HIIT with cycling will make working out more enjoyable. Aside from being able to workout at home with a stationary bike, you will also become ready for long distance biking trips. As you gain more experience as a road cyclist, you may even one day, be able to do a cross-country challenge. All that starts by using the HIIT system in your workout routine.

It's time for you to become an amazing cyclist and athlete. This book also touches on other types of workout that allow you to create a well balanced physique. We also enumerate all the nutrients that you need to develop your muscles. By practicing the principle of balanced workouts and diet suggested by this book, you will gain just enough muscle mass to look good and feel good.

# Chapter 1: HIIT vs. Endurance (Which One Is Better?)

We've seen many hyped exercise regimens come and go. Many of them have promised fast results but only a few could deliver on their promises. Many of you who are reading this book have tried many of these hyped exercise routines. HIIT is not just hyped. It has consistently lived up to its reputation in dealing with fat and losing weight.

HIIT or high intensity interval training is becoming the mainstream cardiovascular workout for many professional athletes. In the past, it was only practiced by track athletes to prepare their muscles for both long distance and short distance runs. Now, boxers, basketball players, and football players are only a few of the professional athletes who integrated HIIT into their workout system.

How to do it?

HIIT can be applied in many types of exercises. You can do it while running or even when lifting weights. Many boxers also use this type of training to simulate their bursts of energy in the ring. Here is an example of a HIIT regimen:

Warm ups:

To effectively execute HIIT, you first need to do warm up exercises at moderate intensity. Many athletes do their warm-ups at 60% intensity. We will discuss how you can calculate your intensity later in the book.

High intensity phase

After warming up, you can now start with the high intensity workout for a period of time. In running, you do this by sprinting at full speed. The same goes when you are cycling. When boxing, you can do this by throwing your combinations as fast as you can without stopping.

Low intensity phase

After the high intensity phase, you then slow down the pace to catch your breath. If you are totally out of breath after the high intensity workout, you can use this time to take a break. The total duration of the slow intensity workout depends on your level of fitness. For beginner cyclists, a 1:5 or 1:6 high intensity to low intensity ratio is a good starting routine. That means that a 10 second sprint on your exercise bike will be followed by 50 or 60 second low intensity cycling.

Repetition

After that duration, you need to repeat the high intensity and low intensity parts again; following the same length of time. Repeating this 4-5 times will make the routine more challenging. You should take a 3 minute break and do the process all over again.

This example of HIIT is for beginners who have not done any workouts for a while. The 1:5 or 1: 6 high intensity and low intensity ratio may seem easy for most seasoned gym goers. We will discuss the specific details of how to do HIIT later in the book.

How is HIIT better?

One of the best ways to show the advantages of using HIIT is by comparing it with workout regimens that have been proven by time. Endurance training is the most used workout regimen around the world. Every time somebody wants to lose weight through workouts, they take out their jogging or cycling gear and hit the road.

There are a lot of studies that answered questions about how well HIIT stacks with its traditional counterpart. Here are some of the areas where HIIT is a better option that regular endurance training.

Studies demonstrated that HIIT is a much better workout routine for burning fat than steady state endurance exercises. A study on the effects of a 15-week HIIT on the fat mass of young women showed that HIIT is more effective in getting rid of fats than regular steady state endurance exercises. Those who underwent HIIT had significant improvements on their total body mass, fat mass, trunk fat and fasting plasma insulin levels.

The benefits of HIIT are greatly increased in fit and athletic people. People who are living a sedentary lifestyle may require a moderate version of High Intensity Interval Cycling training to be able to build their resistance.

Athletic performance is difficult to improve once it reached a certain level. Most athletes experience a plateau in speed, strength and endurance improvement when they train. They put in more training hours doing traditional endurance workouts but they don't feel the same improvement rates that they experienced in the past. HIIT's different approach allows them to get past this plateau and see more improvements in their cardiovascular fitness. If you are an experienced cyclist and you want to further improve your skills, HIIT is also a good option for you to try.

A 2008 study showed that HIIT training for two hours and thirty minutes has the same benefits as 10-hour endurance training in terms of biochemical changes in the muscles and cardio-respiratory endurance benefits. Studies also show that the resting metabolic rate or RMR of people who undergo HIIT is increased compared to people who do the same duration of endurance training. This means that people who use HIIT burn more fats naturally after the workout than people who use regular endurance training.

More studies are still being conducted to explore how the high and low intensity training combination affects the overall cardio-respiratory and muscle health.

## Chapter 2: You Can HIIT on the Bike, Did You Know That?

High intensity interval training is becoming popular as an endurance workout substitute for people who want to try something new. It is usually applied to resistance training and running.

Few people know however, that HIIT can also be done in a workout bicycle. Cyclists and fitness buffs alike love using HIIT as a part of their training regimen because it breaks the monotony of steady-pace endurance workouts. For cyclists, the high intensity training improves their sprinting performance. For the everyday workout Joe and Jane, HIIT on a bike is a good workout regimen for losing weight and body fat.

To be able to start using HIIT on your bike, you need to gather your biking equipment and gear. Having the complete workout gear will motivate you to work harder. You will also love using your smart phone as a workout tool. There are apps that you can use that will measure all types of workout analytics for you. Some of these apps will be discussed in detail later in the book

If you are lucky enough to have some outdoor area where you can use an actual bike, you will also need outdoor equipment that will make your cycling trips safer and more comfortable. You also need to learn the basics of repairing a bike on the road. There are a lot of innovative tools available out there but they will all be worthless if you don't learn how to use them properly.

Starting Out

If you haven't been on the road in your bike for a while, you might want to start putting some time on your stationary bike. This will prepare your muscles for the road work ahead. It will also allow you to gauge your endurance when sprinting.

The basic idea behind HIIT is to do alternating high intensity and low intensity workout. In biking, you need to sprint during the high intensity part of the workout. You should then do moderate cycling speeds for a short period of time. You should do these two degrees of cycling intensity a number of times to effectively execute HIIT.

Using New Muscle Types

By alternating the intensity of your movements, you will be activating both fast twitch and slow twitch muscle fibers in your legs and your lower backs.

Slow twitch muscle fibers

This type of muscle fiber is effective in using oxygen efficiently. It is used in extended muscle use like biking long distances at moderate speed. In slow continuous movements, the muscles have enough time to burn oxygen to keep up with the energy requirement of the task. Using this type of muscle prevents lactic acid formation which causes the feeling of muscle fatigue and pain.

Fast twitch muscle fibers

This type of muscles is used for explosive actions. When we do high intensity workouts, our body compensates with the energy requirements of our movements by using anaerobic metabolism. This allows the body to release short bursts of energy.

This is the type of muscle fibers that we use when we sprint in our exercise bike. Anaerobic respiration however, creates and accumulates lactic acid. This is the cause of our muscle pain when we prolong our sprint.

The level of difficulty of high intensity interval training can be adjusted depending on your level of fitness. We can adjust this factor by increasing or decreasing the ratio between high and low intensity trainings. In the previous chapter, we gave an example where there is a 50 or 60 second low intensity workout period for every 10 seconds of high intensity training.

If you have been living a sedentary lifestyle before starting to workout, you may need to adjust the duration of the sprints. A good starting point is to do explosive sprinting on your exercise bike for 5-8 seconds. You can then do moderate speed cycling in the next 60 seconds. You should do this 8 times.

As you grow stronger and as your sprinting endurance improves, you can move to increase the high intensity training and decrease the low intensity phase.

Working on the road

When working out on the road, you should make sure that you are using a road safe enough for bike sprinting. The ideal road for sprinting is a low traffic road with few or no intersections. There are should also be no buildings near the street. Buildings create blindsides where a car may come out of nowhere while you are sprinting. You need to make sure that the road ahead is clear before you sprint. If your town hosts regular cycling events, you can use the routes used by these events.

# Chapter 3: Weekly Trainings to Get Stronger, Faster, Lighter

The HIIT cycling program that will be discussed in the following chapter will be divided into three stages; the beginner, intermediate, and expert stages. For best results, you need to choose the stage that is appropriate for your level of fitness.

The beginner stage

This stage is perfect for people who have been living a sedentary lifestyle prior to the HIIT program. It is focused on improving your cardiovascular health to prepare you for the next stages of the program. Just like in any beginner workout program, the beginner stage of the High Intensity Interval Cycling Training will have a long warm-up period. It also has longer durations for the low intensity part of the training.

After the beginner stage, you will have muscles that are ready for the later stages. The muscles that have weakened because of the sedentary lifestyle will become ready for more rigorous types of workout tasks. In this stage, there will already be a short duration of high intensity biking. These short sprints will activate your fast twitch muscles. This type of muscles fibers is the least used by people who are living a sedentary lifestyle. People who are not accustomed to sprinting often expose these muscles to injury when they instantly expose them to high intensity workouts. Through this stage, you will allow them to start working with the minimal risk of injury. The long warm-up periods will also allow this type of muscles to heat up and become more flexible before they are exposed to sprinting.

You should also take into consideration that you will be experiencing some muscle pains due to the lactic acid accumulation in the muscles. This may happen after sprinting and may linger on after the workout. This type of pain may be paralyzing at first but as you become more familiar with the sensation, you will become desensitized from it. Many bikers experience the same thing and they have developed a tolerance to the pain caused by the process. Your aim is to develop the same type of tolerance in your beginner stage.

This stage is also designed to make you feel comfortable with breathing while you are on the bike. Breathing is the key to longer performances. In the beginning, you will struggle to catch your breath after sprints. As you become more experienced, your breathing will be able to transition between sprints and low intensity speeds smoothly.

Breathing is most important during the low intensity phase of the workout. This is the time for aerobic respiration. At this phase, you should keep your mind focused in your breathing. People who take their breathing for granted in this stage often take shallow breaths resulting to a lack of oxygen in their inhalation. Their body will try to compensate for the lack of oxygen by breathing faster. The fast breathing combined with inadequate supply of oxygen will cause them to tire faster.

For a longer performance, you should practice doing deep regular breathing. During aerobic respiration, your body will be producing a lot carbon dioxide. Deep exhalation allows your body to release the carbon dioxide faster. Deep breathing during the low intensity phase of the workout also prevents the body from relying on anaerobic respiration. This will lessen the amount of lactic acid accumulation in your muscles.

You will only do this workout 3x a week. This will give you more time to do other types of workouts on the other days of the week. It will also give your thigh and calf muscles time to heal for the next HIIT biking session. The 3-day weekly workout will increase the rate of your metabolism. Exercise naturally increases that but it begins to slow down again 24 hours after working out. By working out every other day, your metabolism will have no time to slow down. Maintaining a fast metabolic rate will help you burn more fats when you are in your rested state.

| Day of the week | HIIT Program |
|---|---|
| Monday | Warm up for 8 minutes: Your normal biking pace<br><br>Resistance: Low<br><br>Rest: 2 minutes<br><br>Workout:<br><br>10 seconds high intensity (sprints), 1 minute low intensity (repeat 6 times)<br><br>Rest: 1 minute<br><br>10 seconds high intensity (sprints), 1 minute low intensity (repeat 6 times)<br><br>Total workout time: 25 minutes |
| Tuesday | Strength training day |
| Wednesday | Warm up for 8 minutes: Your normal biking pace<br><br>Resistance: Low<br><br>Rest: 2 minutes<br><br>Workout:<br><br>10 seconds high intensity (sprints), 1 |

| | |
|---|---|
| | minute low intensity (repeat 6 times) |
| | Rest: 1 minute |
| | 10 seconds high intensity (sprints), 1 minute low intensity (repeat 6 times) |
| | Total workout time: 25 minutes |
| Thursday | Strength training day |
| Friday | Warm up for 8 minutes: Your normal biking pace |
| | Resistance: Low |
| | Rest: 2 minutes |
| | Workout: |
| | 15 seconds high intensity (sprints), 1 minute low intensity (repeat 6 times) |
| | Rest: 1 minute |
| | 15 seconds high intensity (sprints), 1 minute low intensity (repeat 6 times) |
| | Total workout time: 25 minutes |
| Saturday | Strength training day |
| Sunday | Rest day |

You should do this workout routine for one month. Unlike regular endurance training, HIIT routines don't need 45 minutes to burn fats. You need to focus more on improving the power in your sprints and keeping your breathing regular.

After one month, you could now try the workout routine of the intermediate stage. If you become out of breath while doing it, you can spend some more time using the beginner stage routine until your endurance has developed for the next level.

Intermediate stage

You can start with the intermediate stage after your first month. In this stage, the intensity of the workout will begin to increase. There will be shorter warm-up and rest periods. In the previous stage, the high intensity-low intensity ratio was 10 seconds is to 1 minute or 1:6. On the Friday sessions, we increased it to 15 seconds is to 1 minute or 1:4. In this stage we will bring them closer and make the workout a bit more challenging.

At the end of this stage, your calf and thigh muscles will significantly improve. These muscles will become more accustomed to generating busts of energy. You will be more accustomed to sprinting and your tolerance towards the pain caused by the lactic acid will also increase.

The longer duration of the workout sessions will also significantly increase your cardio-respiratory resistance. Combined with the proper deep breathing method during the low intensity phase of the workout, you will be able to last longer during workouts. Improving your resistance for long rides will prepare your body for the time when you will start working out on the road.

In this stage, we will also introduce the super set. A super set is a workout session that is longer than your usual duration. You do this when you still feel like working out even after your usual routine is done. It could also include a closer high intensity-low intensity ratio.

The HIIT superset will help you burn fat much faster. After the first 20 minutes of workout, your body will begin tapping into your energy reserves. This is the reason behind your fat loss. Most of the time, the fat loss will come from your tummy or your chest. Using a super set will prolong the duration that your body is using your fat reserves. This will result to more fat loss per session when compared to your regular workout.

Because the duration and the intensity of the workout in a HIIT superset are increased, you may need more time to recover from it. In our Monday-Wednesday-Friday workout schedule, the best time to do it is on Friday. This will give your calf and thigh muscles more time to recover before the next HIIT bike session.

| Day of the week | HIIT Program |
|---|---|
| Monday | Warm up for 5 minutes: Your normal biking pace<br><br>Resistance: Low<br><br>Rest: 1 minutes<br><br>Workout:<br><br>30 seconds high intensity (sprints), 1 minute low intensity (repeat 8 times)<br><br>Rest: 1 minute<br><br>30 seconds high intensity (sprints), 1 minute low intensity (repeat 5 times) |

|  | Total workout time: 26 minutes and 30 seconds |
|---|---|
| Tuesday | Strength training day |
| Wednesday | Warm up for 5 minutes: Your normal biking pace<br><br>Resistance: Low<br><br>Rest: 1 minutes<br><br>Workout:<br><br>30 seconds high intensity (sprints), 1 minute low intensity (repeat 8 times)<br><br>Rest: 1 minute<br><br>30 seconds high intensity (sprints), 1 minute low intensity (repeat 5 times)<br><br>Total workout time: 26 minutes and 30 seconds |
| Thursday | Strength training day |
| Friday | Warm up for 5 minutes: Your normal biking pace<br><br>Resistance: Low<br><br>Rest: 1 minutes<br><br>Workout:<br><br>30 seconds high intensity (sprints), 1 minute low intensity (repeat 8 times)<br><br>Rest: 1 minute<br><br>40 seconds high intensity (sprints), 1 minute low intensity (repeat 5 times)<br><br>Total workout time: 27 minutes |
| Saturday | Strength training day |
| Sunday | Rest day |
| Superset Day | Warm up for 10 minutes: Your normal biking pace |

| | |
|---|---|
| | Resistance: Medium |
| | Rest: 1 minutes |
| | Workout: |
| | Resistance: Low |
| | 30 seconds high intensity (sprints), 1 minute low intensity (repeat 5 times) |
| | Rest: 1 minute |
| | 30 seconds high intensity (sprints), 1 minute low intensity (repeat 5 times) |
| | Rest: 1 minute |
| | 40 seconds high intensity (sprints), 1 minute low intensity (repeat 3 times) |
| | Total workout time: 33 minutes |

If you don't have a lot of experience being on a bike, you should stay on the intermediate stage for at least 2 months. You should try to narrow down the high intensity-low intensity ratio to make the routine more challenging.

If you are in a country with a hot climate, you will sweat a lot especially when doing a super set. You should have energy bars and energy drinks ready in case of dehydration and hypoglycemia.

Expert stage

Before you move on to the expert, you should make sure that you are ready for long distance biking because this is the stage where you will go out on the road. When you are on the road, you should remember to reserve some energy for the trip back. Start with small distance rides and increase your distance on each trip.

You should also know the basics of going on a cycling trip. You should plan out your route to get back home on time. Sprinting on your bike is not a good idea in the busy city streets. You should make sure that the route you take will be free of heavy traffic and pedestrians. If you have bike lanes in your city streets, you should focus your route on those lanes.

The expert stage is a combination of stationary bike and road workouts. The amount of road workout that you do depends on how much time you can devote to it. If you are a weekend warrior, you should plan your weekend around your road biking sessions.

In this stage, you should follow the routine of the intermediate stage. You should then add a superset after the day's routine. You should try to finish the superset or push until you are out of air.

| Day of the week | HIIT Program |
|---|---|
| Monday | Intermediate Stage Routine |
| | Super Set |
| Tuesday | Strength training day |
| Wednesday | Intermediate Stage Routine |
| | Super Set |
| Thursday | Strength training day |
| Friday | Intermediate Stage Routine |
| | Super Set |
| Saturday | Strength training day |
| Sunday | Rest day |
| Superset Day | Warm up for 10 minutes: Your normal biking pace |
| | Resistance: Medium |
| | Rest: 1 minutes |
| | Workout: |
| | Resistance: Low |
| | 30 seconds high intensity (sprints), 1 minute low intensity (repeat 5 times) |
| | Rest: 1 minute |
| | 30 seconds high intensity (sprints), 1 minute low intensity (repeat 5 times) |
| | Rest: 1 minute |
| | 40 seconds high intensity (sprints), 1 minute low intensity (repeat 3 times) |
| | Total workout time: 33 minutes |

On the road, you should find the best leg in your route where you can sprint. Use the intermediate stage routine while travelling in this part of the route. You should avoid places however, that have a lot of sharp turns. You should also avoid doing HIIT routines on areas that have a lot of cliffs. Highways in plains outside of the urban areas are the best type of road to use your bike in.

# Chapter 4: Working Out Beyond The Bike - Let's Build Some Muscle

In the previous chapter, we showed you how to do HIIT using your bike. That bike routine is perfect for improving your cardio-respiratory health and increasing the resistance will significantly improve your leg strength. However, it will have very little effect on your arms and upper body strength.

This is the reason why we have strength training in our chart in the previous chapter. On each strength training day, you will work on a different pair of muscle groups. With cycling HIIT, you will burn fats faster. The fat mass in your arms, your gut and your chest will be replaced with muscles giving you a chiseled physique.

To develop a balanced physique, you also need to put some gym time building your upper body strength. In this chapter, we will discuss how you will be able to improve the muscles size and strength in your abdomen, chest, shoulders and upper back. Doing so will also improve the strength in your arms.

The HIIT principle can also be applied to your muscle building routines. To avoid injuries, you must work on different muscle groups every day. By doing this, you will be able to build your muscles in different areas of the body each week. Each muscle group will also have time for repairs before they are used again.

To start your HIIT on building muscles, you need to identify the right weight to use. If you haven't tried using a barbell or a dumbbell in your life, do the following workouts on the various weights suggested. If you could do 10 reps with ease, then you should move on to the next weight level. The objective is to find the best weight where you can consistently do 10 proper repetitions

| Type of Exercise | Target Muscle Group | Weight Level 1 | Weight Level 2 | Weight Level 3 | Weight Level 4 |
|---|---|---|---|---|---|
| Bench Press | Chest | 30 pounds | 40 pounds | 50 pounds | 60 pounds |
| Isolated Dumbbell Curls | Biceps | 15 pounds | 20 pounds | 25 pounds | 30 pounds |
| One-arm Triceps Extension | Triceps | 10 pounds | 15 pounds | 20 pounds | 30 pounds |
| Barbell Dead Lift | Back | 30 pounds | 40 pounds | 50 pounds | 60 pounds |

After finding out the optimum starting weight to use, you need to practice the proper way of execution for each of the exercise movements suggested below. The cheapest way to do this is by looking for exercise videos online. There are a lot of exercise gurus who will show you how to do the exercises properly to avoid injuries. Practice each weight training move before moving on to the HIIT strength program.

Here are the strength training moves that you need to work on:

1. Seated Isolated Dumbbell Curls

2. Barbell Squats

3. One Arm Triceps Extension

4. Stationary Lunge

5. Hammer Curls

6. Triceps Kickback

7. Bench Press

8. Bent Over Barbell Row (Wide Grip)

9. Lying Fly

10. Incline Dumbbell Bench press

11. Barbell Dead Lift

12. Wide Grip Bench Press

13. Crunches

14. Leg Raise

15. Barbell Trunk Rotation

You don't have to learn all of them instantly. You could look them up one by one as the need arises.

Some of these workout moves require a spotter or a partner during working out. You should ask a friend to spot for you if you are working out at home. The gym instructor will usually be the spotter if you are a gym member.

Because you only have 3 workout days left with one rest day, you should work on two muscle groups on each training day. Here are the groups that you need to work on each day:

| Day | Pair of Muscle Groups |
|---|---|
| Tuesday | Arms and Legs |
| Thursday | Back and Chest |
| Saturday | Abdominal Muscles and Arms |

Most men like having big arms. This is the reason why we work on our arms twice every week. You can replace the arm muscle group with any other muscle group that you want to grow faster and stronger.

Here's the HIIT workout plan that you can follow using the arrangement above:

| Day | Workout | Target Muscle Group | Weight | Number of reps | Intensity |
|---|---|---|---|---|---|
| Tuesday | Seated Isolated Dumbbell Curls | Biceps | 60% of optimum weight | 10 | High |
| | Barbell Squats | Legs | optimum weight | 10 | Low |
| | One Arm Triceps Extension | Triceps | 60% of optimum weight | 10 | High |
| | 1-minute Rest | | | | |
| | Stationary Lunge | Legs | Bodyweight | 10 | High |
| | Hammer Curls | Biceps | optimum weight | 10 | Low |
| | Triceps Kickback | Triceps | 60% of optimum weight | 10 | High |
| | | | | | |
| Thursday | Bench Press | Chest | 50% of optimum | 10 | High |

|  |  |  |  |  |  |
|---|---|---|---|---|---|
|  |  |  | weight |  |  |
|  | Bent Over Barbell Row (Wide Grip) | Back | Optimum Weight | 10 | Low |
|  | Lying Fly | Chest | 60% of optimum weight | 10 | High |
|  | 1 minute rest |  |  |  |  |
|  | Incline Dumbbell Bench press | Chest | 60% of optimum weight | 10 | High |
|  | Barbell Dead Lift | Back | Optimum Weight | 10 | Low |
|  | Wide Grip Bench Press | Chest | 50% of optimum weight | 10 | High |
|  |  |  |  |  |  |
| Saturday | Crunches | Abdominal Muscles | Bodyweight | 10 | High |
|  | Seated Isolated Dumbbell Curls | Biceps | optimum weight | 10 | Low |
|  | Leg Raise | Abdominal Muscles | Bodyweight | 10 | High |
|  | 1-minute rest |  |  |  |  |
|  | Hammer Curls | Biceps | 60% of optimum weight | 10 | High |
|  | Barbell Trunk Rotation | Abdominal Muscles | Optimum Weight | 10 | Low |
|  | Triceps Kickback | Triceps | 60% of optimum weight | 10 | High |

To properly execute the HIIT for muscle building, you need to finish the 10 reps of each exercise as fast as you can and move on to the next workout move in the list without resting. As you continue your strength training, the weight will become easier to handle. To keep the workout challenging, you should constantly try out heavier weights.

High intensity weight lifting burns a lot of calories. You will lose a lot of weight if you don't replace the calories that you use up by eating. To build your muscles properly, you need the right combination of carbohydrates and protein. This topic will be discussed later in the book.

# Chapter 5: Welcome To Cycling 2.0 (Gadgets, Apps & More)

When you do venture out into the open road, you should make sure that you are ready for anything. You need be aware of your body condition at all times. You should also anticipate problems that may happen on the road and take measures to prepare for them. Here are some of the things that you will need for your cycling hobby:

Road Bike

The best type of bicycle for you is a road bike. These are built for speed and toughness. They are not as tough as mountain bikes but most of the good brands of road bikes can carry you and the equipment in your back for long distances.

Navigation gadgets

If you are travelling in an unfamiliar area, having a standalone GPS device will prevent you from getting lost. A lot of people argue that you should just bring your smart phone with you and use the built-in GPS. However, phones are pretty fragile and may break with minor bumps on the trip. It's safer to have 2 navigational gadgets with you.

Smart phone

Your smart phone will enhance your biking experience. Using free and paid apps, you will be able to track your trips, the distances you covered, and even the calories you burned. You could even share your workout stats with your friends on social media. Here are some of the apps that allow you to do all these and more:

Map My Ride GPS Cycling Riding

This app on Android allows you to record everything about your cycling performance. It allows you to navigate your route, measure your pace, use the GPS feature of your phone, measure the distance you've travelled for the day, and even present some of the data in sleek looking graphs. It is available in free and paid versions. The paid or MVP version features a real time locator that allows you friends and family to find you during your trips, a heart rate data analyzer and all the other features in the free version without the ads. They also have goal setting feature in the website that recommends are personal training plan available for paying users.

Strava Running and Cycling GPS

This app has similar features as the one above but it has the added feature of making your hobby social. Aside from being able to share your activities to your social media accounts, you will also be able to compare your performance with an online leader board. If you like competition, this is the app for you.

Size My Bike

This is a paid app that allows you to learn about the right bike size for your body dimensions. If you are planning to buy a new road bike, this app will be able to help you find the one that has the best fit for you. Finding the right bike will make your trips more comfortable.

Pro Cycling News

If you are hooked to the world of pro cycling, you should consider using this app. It's free and it aggregates the best cycling news as they are reported by online sources using RSS feeds. It also includes tweeter feeds of cycling's big names.

Basic bike repair tools

You should also have these tools with you especially when on a long distance trip:

Lights

Repair kits

Inner tube repair kit

Spare tube

Air pumps

Spare brake blocks

Spare break cables

Chain breaker

Extra spokes

Allen wrenches of various sizes

Lube

You should learn how to use these tools and spare parts by attending a bike repair class or by learning through the internet. There are a lot of Youtube videos devoted to this subject.

Safety

Safety is the number one reason for all this preparation. You will be able to prevent most of the problems by planning your trips ahead of time.

Planning

While planning a cycling trip, you need to consider the following factors:

### Route

You should memorize where you are going and all the landmarks that you need to pass through. If you enjoy going fast, you should plan to go through roads that are good for sprinting. This means that you need to avoid road types that are prone to accidents.

### Rest stops

You should also consider where you will take a break. You could take a break anywhere in the wilderness but it is much better if you can find some comfortable areas along your route where you can avail of some modern commodities.

### Food and water

Some of the things that you need to consider are food and water. For day trips, you just need to learn what restaurants are in your route. You don't have to worry too much about gaining weight or fat if you eat too much because you will easily burn the food you eat during these trips.

Water is a bigger problem especially in long trips. Carrying too much water will increase the weight in your back significantly. To effectively manage your water intake, drink a lot of water in your planned rest stops. Never forget to fill up your containers before leaving. Try to conserve water in the early parts of the leg.

### Repair shops along the way

You should also consider the possibility of your bike breaking down. There are some types of repairs that cannot be handled by your repair kit. If you are just biking around your home town, you can easily locate a good bike or welding shop to get your bicycle repaired. In long cross country trips however, you need to be able to locate the nearest repair shop.

Fortunately, we have the internet to help us out with that one. Plot out your trip in a map and mark where the nearest repair shops are. Make sure that they are open on the days that you will be in town.

### Weather and wind

Just like in planning any outdoor occasion, you will need to plan for the weather. Try to avoid areas that are prone to landslides during the rainy season. You should also avoid steep downhill slopes on these days. Your clothing will also depend greatly on the weather forecast for your trip. Learn as much as you can about this factor to avoid being underdressed for the occasion.

The wind is also an important factor for cyclists. Some areas with strong gusts will sweep you off the road. Riding against the wind requires a lot more effort and it will tire you out easily. You may not be able to stick to your itinerary because of an unforeseen series of headwinds. When researching about the wind, you should consider the area's reputation and the time of the year.

First Aid Kit

You should also carry a first aid kit equipped with bandages and solutions for wounds and medications for common types of illnesses. In long trips, these medications can be life savers.

Camping equipment for long trips

If you plan to spend the night in the wilderness, you need to be prepared with the right camping equipment. The key to choosing the right equipment is portability. When choosing your tent for instance, you should make sure that it does not take up a lot of space and it is easy to carry.

Clothing and safety gear

Good quality cycling shorts

Not wearing the right clothing may result to damaged skin due to friction with the fabric. This usually happens in the groin area where the skin makes contact with the chair. To avoid these types of injuries, you should make sure that you wear certified cycling shorts with padding.

Helmet and pads

The best types of helmets for road cycling are the aerodynamic cycling helmets or aero helmets. Their shape allows the wind to pass smoothly and minimize the wind resistance. You should also use cycling clothes with built in pads to protect you from crashes.

Rain gear

You could also add a rain jacket during the rainy season. Cycling through the cold may lower your immune system. Using a cycling rain jacket will maintain a warm temperature in your torso even in the rain.

Don't leave home without the following:

Insurance

Make sure that your insurance covers cycling related accidents. Being active outdoors may be seen by some insurance companies as an added risk. Make sure that your hospitalization and life is covered by adding the necessary policy riders.

Let people at home know where you are going

Before leaving home, you should also tell the people you live with where you are going and how long you will be gone. If you can't arrive on time, you should let them know about it through a phone call or an SMS.

# Chapter 6: Supplements & Proper Diet Will Take You Far

To have a healthy body there are three essential factors that you need to take into consideration. First, you need to work out regularly. You should then make sure that you get an adequate amount of rest. This will help your body and mind recover from training and all your other activities. Lastly, you need to constantly refuel your body with the right nutrients. As mentioned in the previous chapter, you need to achieve a balance between carbohydrates and protein to achieve the body that you want.

Carbohydrates

This is one of the major components of your food. Some examples of foods rich in carbohydrates are pasta, bread, wheat and rice. Carbohydrates are important for athletes because they are the best source for energy for our body. It is literally the fuel that keeps us moving.

Protein

Protein on the other hand is the type of nutrients that our body uses to build its most important parts. The majority of the solid parts of your body are made up of protein including your hair, nails and skin.

For athletes, protein is necessary when building muscles. When we work out, we wear our muscles out and this signals our body that our muscles need to improve and become stronger in case it will face similar tasks in the future. In the process of repairing our muscles fibers, it will load up on the available protein. This leads to stronger and bigger muscles.

The right eating time

As an athlete, you have to eat an adequate amount of both protein and carbohydrates to make you ready for the following day's workout. Many people work hard in the gym but are afraid to eat afterwards in the fear of gaining back the weight they lost.

When you eat a big meal, your body cannot use up all the carbohydrates that you take in. Your body will convert the carbohydrates into a state that allows it to be stored. This is the reason most people living a sedentary lifestyle becomes fat. They eat more carbohydrate than they can use up. As a result, most of the carbohydrates that they eat go to their hips, love handles or chest.

Many athletes and celebrities who like to keep in shape have adapted an eating system that allows them to use up all the energy from the carbohydrates without decreasing the amount of food that they take in. The secret is eating six small meals a day rather than 3 big meals. The meals need to be distributed evenly throughout the day to make sure that the previous batch is digested before more is added.

The most crucial times for nutrition in your day are before and after your workout. You will need a good amount of carbohydrates and protein during workout which means that you need to eat one of your six meals 1 hour before your workout. Adding this meal into your day will prevent you from passing out during your workout.

After your workout, it is time for your body to recuperate and repair any damages. At this point it will be looking for structural materials that it will use to build your muscles. This is the best time to load up on protein and a little bit of carbohydrates. If you don't have a regular source of protein from the foods in your fridge, you may need to use whey protein powder. It is the most efficient source of protein because it does not contain fat. You could also use amino acid supplements to keep up with your protein needs.

Make sure to consult with your doctor before taking any high protein products

Supplements

Aside from the two macro minerals mentioned above, you will also need other types of nutrients. One of the nutrient types that you need is vitamins. Vitamins are not an energy source. However, they help make the processes of energy production go faster. You will not become stronger or faster by taking vitamin supplements but if you become deficient of any of them, your performance will suffer. Here are some of the vitamins that you need to take:

Vitamin B Complex

Vitamin B1, B2, and B6 have important roles in the conversion of food energy into chemical energy usable by the body. Vitamins B2, B6, B12 and Folate are also important in the formation of red blood cells. These cells carry oxygen from the lungs to the tissues and cells.

Niacin is one of the most important nutrients for athletes who use the HIIT system. Getting 16 mg of it every day for men and 14 mg for women will regulate your transition period between the use of aerobic and anaerobic respiration.

Vitamin C

This vitamin is world famous as a potent anti oxidant. It has a range of purposes that improves our body's capacity to protect itself from damage and do the necessary repairs. One of its most important functions for athletes is its aid in iron absorption. Iron is a major component of the muscles and the blood. Taking vitamin C together with the B complex vitamins will help prevent athletes from becoming anemic.

As you increase the frequency of your workouts, you will need more vitamin C for maintaining your metabolism.

Vitamin D

Workouts put a lot of stress on our bones. Vitamin D is one of the important nutrients responsible for keeping our bones strong. You can get enough vitamin D by getting a moderate amount of sunlight every day.

Minerals

Minerals on the other hand, are basic elements needed by our body in minute amounts that are important for the function of your body. Here are some of them:

Iron

As mentioned above, Iron is required in many aspects of health that are important to athletes. For instance, it is an essential part of hemoglobin. This is the part of the red blood cells that carries the oxygen. Not having enough iron will lead to anemia.

Zinc

Zinc is another important mineral for athletes that aids in the building and repair of muscles. It is best to take zinc after your workouts to maximize its effects on your muscles. Other than that, zinc also improves our immune system and helps in the production of energy.

Electrolytes

The minerals potassium, chloride and sodium are essential during your workouts or biking trips. These three help our nerves in performing their function. They are usually found in most energy drinks. A deficiency of these three minerals during your workouts will lead dizziness, nausea and even passing out. These are major signs of dehydration.

# Conclusion

Thank you again for downloading this book!

I hope this book was able to help you to learn about the amazing High Intensity Internal Training system.

The next step is to use the principles and knowledge found in this book in practice. The most important part of reaching a workout goal is the journey. Share your workout success with the important people in your life. When you are in the road, take some time to enjoy the scenery of your country or the places that you are visiting.

Finally, if you enjoyed this book, please take the time to share your thoughts and post a review on Amazon. It'd be greatly appreciated!

Thank you and good luck!

Are your jogging sessions not showing any results? The revolutionary High Intensity Interval Training may be the change in routine that you need. This workout system is one of the most popular workout systems in gyms around the world today. This book will help you learn all about HIIT and how it can be integrated to your cycling hobby.

It also includes nutrition and strength training plans that will make you become stronger. This book encourages a balanced growth using the right way. The HIIT system may promote high intensity workouts but this book makes sure that you do it in a safe way. Using this system, you will be able to develop your cycling skills and build a fit body at the same time.

This book will also help you start your cycling hobby. You can start in your very own living room with an exercise bike. Through this book, you will also learn the different tools that you will need and the safety measures that you need to take in your cycling hobby. Getting fit has never been this fun. Don't miss out on this opportunity to reach your fitness goals. Start your fitness journey today with the HIIT Bike Training Routine.

Made in the USA
Monee, IL
12 March 2023

29715557R00017